SIDE ASPENDOS PERGE

SILLYON • SELEUKIA • MANAVGAT • SELGE

WRITTEN BY

KAYHAN DÖRTLÜK

ARCHAEOLOGIST

WRITTEN BY	: Kayhan DÖRTLÜK, Archeologist
TRANSLATION	: Hayriye BUYAN
PHOTOS BY	: Ahmet ESİN, Bekir Baki AKSU, Tahsin AYDOĞMUŞ, Kadir KIR, Vefa KESKİN
GRAPHIS BY	: Gülten GENÇ
RECONSTRUCTION COLOURING	: Gülten GENÇ
TYPE SET	: Deniz ÇIRA
COLOUR SEPARATION	: IŞIN Repıödüksiyon, ESER Grafik
PUBLISHED and PRINTED	: KESKİN COLOR KARTPOSTALCILIK LTD. ŞTİ. MATBAASI
DISTRIBUTED	: KESKİN COLOR KARTPOSTALCILIK SAN. ve PAZ. A.Ş. Ankara Cad. No.98 34410 SİRKECİ - İSTANBUL Tel : 0 (212) 514 17 47 - 514 17 48 - 514 17 49 Fax: 512 09 64
BRANCH OFFICE	: Kışla Mah. 54. Sk. Günaydın Apt. No: 6/B 07040 ANTALYA Tel: 0 (242) 247 15 41 - 247 16 11 Fax: 247 16 11

ISBN 975-7559-78-4

1997
© copyright by KESKİN COLOR AŞ

CONTENTS

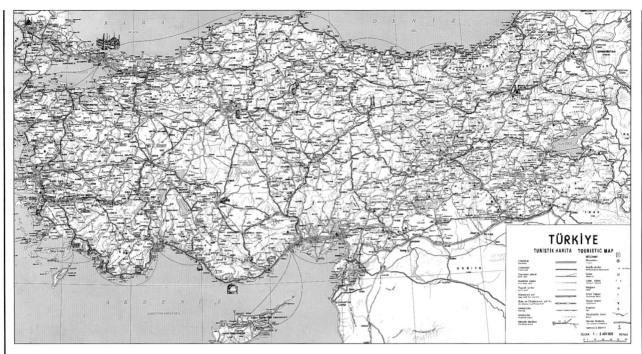

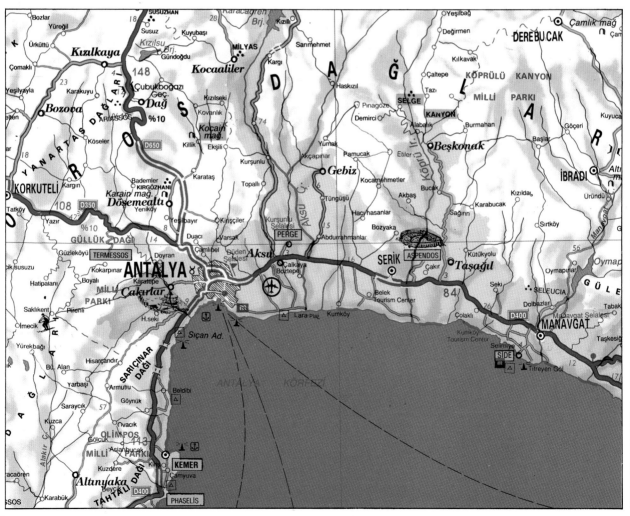

4

PERGE

Perge, one of Pamphylia's foremost cities, was founded on a wide plain between two hills 4 km. west of the Kestros (Aksu) river.

Skylax, who lived in the fourth century B.C. and was the earliest of the ancient writers to mention Perge, states that the city was in Pamphylia. In the New Testament book, Acts of the Apostles, the sentence "... when Paul and his company loosed from Paphos, they came to Perge in Pamphylia" (Acts 13:13), suggests that Perge could be reached from the sea in ancient times. Just as the Kestros provides convenient communication today, the river also played an important role in antiquity, making the land productive, and securing for Perge the possibility of sea trade. Despite its being some 12 km. inland from the sea, Perge by means of the Kestros, was able to benefit from the advantages of the sea as if it were a coastal city. Moreover, it was removed from the attacks of pirates invading by sea.

In later copies of a third or fourth century map of the world, Perge is shown beside the principal road starting at Pergamum and ending at Side.

According to Strabo, the city was founded after the Trojan War by colonists from Argos under the leadership of heroes named Mopsos and Calchas. Linguistic research confirms that Achaeans entered Pamphylia toward the end of the second millennium B.C. In addition to these studies, inscriptions dating to 120-121 A.D., discovered in the 1953 excavations in the courtyard of Perge's Hellenistic city gate, provide further testimony to this colonization; inscriptions on statue bases mention the names of seven heroes-Mopsos, Calchas, Riksos, Labos, Machaon, Leonteus, and Minyasas, the legendary founders of the city.

There is no further record of Perge in written sources until the middle of the fourth century. There can be no doubt, however, that Perge was also under Persian rule until the arrival of Alexander the Great.

In 333 B.C. Perge surrendered to Alexander without resistance. Its submissive behaviour can be explained by, besides its favourable policy, the fact that at this period the city was not yet surounded by protective walls.

With the death of Alexander, Perge remained for a short time within the boundaries of Antigonos domain and later fell under Seleucid sovereignty. When the border dispute between the Seleucids and the king of Pergamum continued after the treaty of Apamea, the Roman consul Manlius Vulso was sent from Rome in 188 A.D. capacity

General view of Perge

PLAN OF PERGE

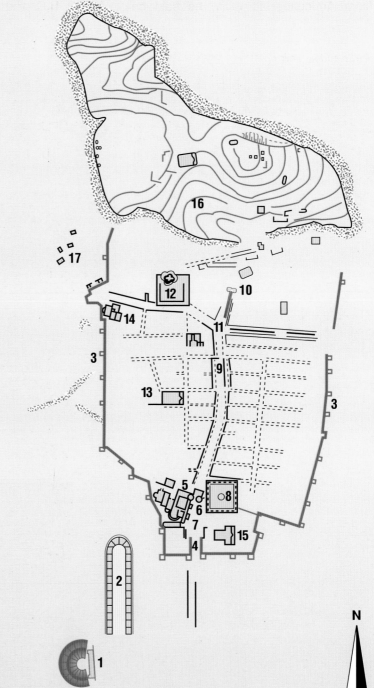

1 THEATRE
2 STADIUM
3 CITY WALLS
4 LATE PERIOD GATEWAY
5 SOUTH BATHS
6 HELLENISTIC GATEWAY
7 FOUNTAIN
8 AGORA
9 COLLONNADED STREET
10 NORTH FOUNTAIN
11 ARCH OF DEMETRIUS
   APOLLONIS
12 PALAESTRA
13 NORTH BASILICA
14 NORTH BATHS
15 WEST BASILICA
16 ACROPOLIS
17 NECROPOLIS

N

of mediator. Learning that Antiochos III had a garrison in Perge, he surrounded the city at the urging of Pergamum's king. At this point the garrison commander informed the consul that he could not surrender the city before obtaining permission from Antiochos; for this, he said he would need thirty days, at the end of which, Perge passed to Pergamum.

Perge became totally independent when the kingdom of Pergamum was turned over to Rome in about 133 B.C.

In 79 B.C. the Roman statesman Cicero de-

Theatre of Perge and a general view of the antique city

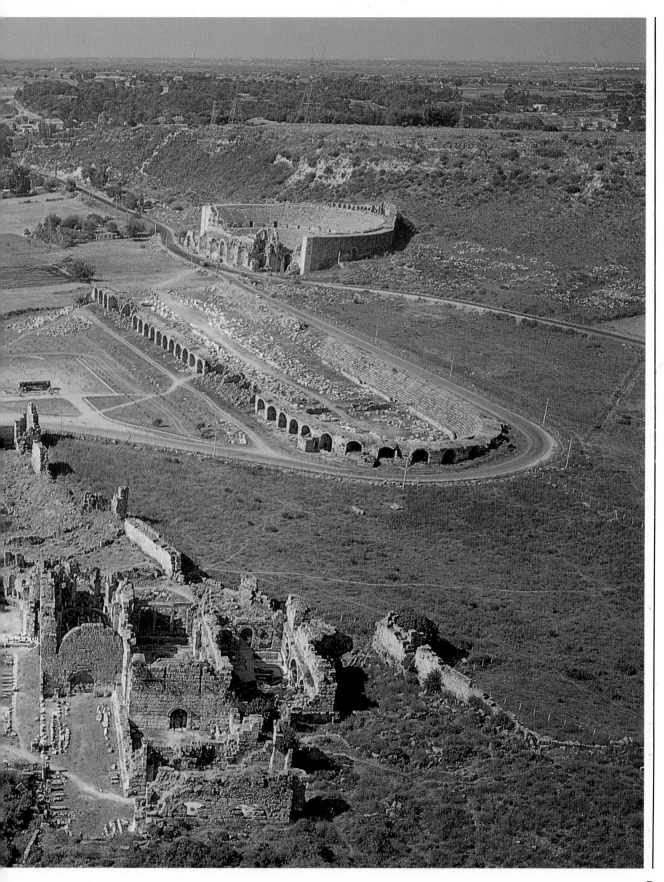

The interior of the Theatre of Perge

scribed to the senate, Cilician questor Gaius Verres' unlawful conduct in Perge, saying, "As you know, there is a very old and sacred temple to Diana in Perge. I assert that this was also robbed and looted by Verres and that the gold was stripped from the statue of Diana and stolen."
Artemis occupied an important position among the gods and goddesses held sacred in Perge. This ancient Anatolian goddess appears on Hellenistic coins under the name Vanassa Preiia, as she was called in the Pamphylian dialect; after Greek colonization she became known as Artemis Pergaia. Besides being rendered on co-

inage as a cult statue or as a huntress, the Artemis of Perge is the subject of a variety of statues and reliefs found in excavations of the city. A relief in the form of a cult statue on a square stone block is particularly interesting. The cult of Artemis Pergaia also appears in many other cities, even in countries around the Mediterranean. As famous as Artemis Pergaia was in the ancient world, no trace of the temple has yet been found. For the present we must content ourselves with what knowledge we can get from schematic representations of the temple on coins; of this renowned monument that safeguarded the gold-adorned statue of Artemis, and whose scale, beauty, and construction was marvelled at by ancient writers.

In 46 A.D., Perge became the setting of an event important to the Christian world. The New Testament book, the Acts of th Apostles, writes that St. Paul journeyed from Cyprus to Perge. from there continued on to Antiocheia in Pisidia, then returned to Perge where he delivered a sermon. Then he left the city and went to Attaleia.

From the beginning of the Imperial era, work projects were carried out in Perge, and in the second and third centuries A.D., the city grew into one of the most beautiful, not just in Pamphylia, but in all of Anatolia.

In the first half of the fourth century, during the reign of Constantine the Great (324-337), Perge became an important centre of Christianity once this faith had became the official religion of the Roman Empire. The city retained its status as a Christian centre in the fifth and sixth centuries. Due to frequent rebellions and raids, the citizens retreated inside the city walls, able to defend themselves only from within the acropolis. Perge lost its remaining power in the wake of the mid-

Antique Roman Bath

Antique Roman Bath

seventh century with Arab raids. At this time some residents of the city migrated to Antalya.

The first building one encounters on entering the city is a theatre of Greco-Roman type constructed on the southern slopes of the Kocabelen hill. The cavea, slightly more than a semicircle, is divided in two by a wide diazoma passing through it. It contains 19 seating levels below and 23 above, which translate into a total seating capacity of about 13,000. In conformance to the canons of Roman theatre galleries serving as the entrance and exit ways, spectators reached the diazoma from the parados on either side via vaulted passages and stairs; from there they were dispersed to their seats.

The orchestra, situated between the cavea and the stage building, is wider than a semicircle. Because of the gladiatorial and wild animal combats popular in the mid-third century, the orchestra was used as an arena. To keep the animals from escaping, it was surrounded by carved balustrade panels that passed between marble knobs made in the form of Herme.

The partially standing two-storey stage building can be dated to the middle of the second century A.D. by its columned architecture and sculptural ornamentation. On the facade, columns between the five doors by which the actors entered and exited support a narrow podium above. The theatre's most striking feature is a series of marble reliefs of mythological subjects decorating the face of this podium. The first relief on the right portrays the local god personifying the Kestros (Aksu) river, Perge's lifeblood, along with one of the mythological females called nymphs. From here on, the reliefs depict, in serial form, the entire life story of Dionysos, the god of wine and the founder and protector of theatres. Dionysos was the son of Zeus and Semele, the daughter of a king and reputed to be as beautiful as spring. Hera, ever jealous of her husband, wanted to get rid of Semele along with her son. To trick her, the goddess assumed the form of the girl's mother and begged Semele to persuade Zeus to let her see him in all his might and glory. The credulous Semele was taken in by the ruse and implored Zeus to acquiesce. Zeus, unable to resist the pleas of his beloved, came

Pediment friezes and architrave blocks of the theatre

A general view of The Theatre of Perge

down from Olympos on his golden chariot and appeared before her, but the mortal Semele could not withstand his radiance and was consumed by fire. Dying, she gave birth to the fruit of her love, who had not yet come to full term, and threw him from the flames. Zeus took this little boy, sewed him into his hip and kept him there until his term was completed. It is in this way that the boy was given the name Dionysos - born once from his mother's womb and coming into the world a second time from his father's hip. So that the infant could be protected from Hera's malevolence, fed and brought to manhood, he was taken by Hermes to the nymphs of Mount Nysa, who raised the boy in a cave, giving him love and careful attention. Finally, as a young man, Dionysos one day drank the juice of all the grapes on the vine growing along the cave's walls. This is how wine was discovered. With the aim of introducing his new drink into every corner of the globe and spreading the knowledge of viniculture, the god of wine went on a journey around the world in a chariot drawn by two panthers.

It is unfortunate that an important section of these beautiful reliefs was damaged as a result of the subsidence of the stage building. From

pieces recovered during excavations begun in 1985, it is evident that the building was originally decorated with several more friezes on different themes. The subject of a 5 metre-long frieze from an as yet undetermined part of the buiding is especially interesting. Here, Tyche holds a cornucopia in her left hand, and in her right a cult statue. On either side are the figures of an old man and two youths bringing bulls for sacrifice to the goddess.

On the right of the asphalt road running from the theatre to the city, is one of the best preserved stadiums to have survived from ancient times to our own. This huge rectangular building measuring 34x334 metres, is shaped like a horseshoe on its north end and open on its south. It is very likely that the building was entered at this point via a monumental wooden door. The stadium was built on a substructure of 70 vaulted chambers, 30 along each long side and 10 on its narrow northern end. These chambers are interconnected, with every third compartment providing entrance to the theatre. From inscriptions over the remaining compartments giving the names of their owners and listing various types of goods, it is clear that these spaces were used as shops. The tiers of seats which lie on top of

these vaulted rooms, provided a seating capacity of 12,000. When gladiatorial and wild animal combat became popular in the mid-third century, the north end of the stadium was surrounded with a protective balustrade and turned into an arena. Its architectural style and stone work date this edifice to the second century A.D.

Another noteworthy ruin outside the city walls is the tomb of Plancia Magna, who was the daughter of Plancius Verus, the Governor of Bithynia. She was a wealthy and civic minded woman who, around the beginning of the second century, was a major contributor to the construction of public works in Perge, and who had a number of spots in the city adorned with monuments and sculpture. Because of her community service, the people, assembly, and senate erected statues of her. In various inscriptions Plancia's name appears with the title ' demiurgos", which was the highest civil servant in the city's government. In addition, she was a priestess of Artemis Pergaia, a priestess-for-life of the mother of the gods, and the head priestess of the cult of the emperor.

A large part of Perge is encircled by walls that in some places go back to the Hellenistic period. Towers 12-13 metres high were built on top of

Frescoes in the Theatre of Perge

Statue of Marsyas, 2nd century A.D.

Northern fountain, Perge

the fortifications. However, during the time of the Pax Romana, which provided a period of continuous peace and tranquility, the walls lost their importance, and buildings such as the theatre and stadium could be built beyond the walls without fear. On entering the city through a late period gate in the fourth century walls, one comes to a small rectangular court 40 metres long bounded by walls of later date. From this courtyard one continues through a second, southern gate built in the form of a triumphal arch and highly decorated, particularly on the back. This gate leads into a trapezoidal courtyard 92 metres long and 46 metres wide. On the west wall of this court, which was used as a ceremonial site during the reign of Emperor Septimius Sev-

Stadium

erus (193-211 A.D.), is a monumental fountain or nymphaeum. The building consists of a wide pool, and behind it a two-storeyed richly worked facade. From its inscription, it is apparent that the structure was dedicated to Artemis Pergaia, Septimius Severus and his wife Julia Domna, and their sons. An inscription belonging to the facade, various facade fragments, and marble statues of Septimius Severus and his wife, all found in excavations of the nymphaeum, are now in the Antalya Museum.

A monumental propylon directly north of the nymphaeum opens onto the largest and most magnificent bath in Pamphylia. A large pool (natacia) measuring 13x20 m. covers the inside of an apsed chamber on the south portico of a broad palaestra; the palaestra is bounded in front by a portico. Pergaians cleansed themselves in this pool after exercising in the palaestra. It is clear from the dynamic architecture of the facade, the coloured marble facing, and the statues of Genius, Heracles, Hygiea, Asklepios and Nemesis, that decorated, this space must have been duzzlingly beautiful. From here another door leads to the frigidarium, a space that also contained a pool. Before entering, bathers washed their feet in water flowing along a shallow channel running the full length of the pool's north side. Existing evidence suggests that the frigidarium was adorned with statues of the

Reconstruction of Hellenistic Gateway, Perge

Roman Gateway

Hellenistic Gateway

Muses. Next are the tepidarium and the caldarium, which connect with each other. Beneath these rooms one can see courses of bricks belonging to the hypocaust system that circulated the hot air coming from the boiler room. Washing in a Roman bath was a process that took place in several stages. First the bather removed his clothing in a room called the apodyterium and from there entered the palaestra where he took his exercise. Then he either went into the pool to get rid of the dirt and perspiration from this physical exertion, or washed himself in hot water in the caldarium. From there he went to the tepidarium or to the frigidarium for a cold water bath. In the Roman era

the bath was not just a place for washing, but was also a place where men met to pass the time of day or to discuss a variety of important topics. The long rectangular compartment at the north of the frigidarium was probably a place where bathers strolled and chatted. A long marble bench extends along this room's west wall. Inscriptions on a large number of plinths found during excavations, indicate the statues that once stood on them were donated by a man named Claudius Peison.

At the northern end of the inner court is a Hellenistic gate that is Perge's most magnificent structure. Dating to the third century B.C., this gate, consisting of two towers with a horseshoe-

A general view of the stadium

shaped court behind them, was cleverly designed according to the defensive strategy of the day. The towers had three storeys and were covered with a conical roof. With the aid of Plancia Magna, several alterations in the decoration of the court were made between 120 and 122 A.D., changing it from a defensive structure to a court of honour. To create a facade, the Hellenistic walls were covered with slabs of coloured marble, several new niches were opened, and Corinthian columns were added. Figures of gods and goddesses like Aphrodite, Hermes, Pan and

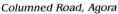

Columned Road, Agora

Columns and Architraveblocks of the Agora

the Dioskouroi occupied the niches on the lower level. In excavations in the court, the inscribed bases of nine statues were found, but the statues themselves have not been recovered. According to their inscriptions, these statues, which must have been placed in the niches on the upper level, represent the legendary heroes who founded Perge after the Trojan War, as described in historical notes. In inscriptions on two pedestals, the names M. Plancius Varus and C. Plancius Varus, his son, appear with the adjective meaning "founder", essentially, because of their goodness and generosity toward Perge, they were accepted as second founders for whom this honour seemed appropriate.

The horseshoe-shaped court is bounded on the north by a three-arched monumental gate built by Plancia Magna. Inscriptions on pedestals unearthed in excavations indicate that statues of

Grave with the figures of Heracles (Museum of Antalya)

Interior view of the Hellenistic Gateway

the emperors and their wives from the reign of Nerva to Hadrian, stood in the gate's niches.

An agora 65 metres square is located to the east of the Hellenistic gate. On all four sides a wide stoa surrounds a central court lined with shops. The floor of these shops is paved with coloured mosaics. An interesting stone used in an ancient game can be seen in front of one store in the north portico. The game, which was played with six stones per person and thrown like dice, must have been very popular throughout the region, as similar stones were also found in other neighbouring cities. At the centre of the court is a round building, just as there is in Side's agora; the precise nature of this structure is not yet known.

A colonnaded street runs north-south through the city centre going under the triumphal arch of Demetrios-Apollonios, currently under restoration, at a point near the acropolis. This thoroughfare is intersected by another running east-west. On both sides of this 250 metre-long street are broad poticoes behind which are rows of shops. In this way the columned architecture on both sides offers various examples of the Roman understanding of perspective. The porticoes also provided a place where people could both take shelter from the violent rains in winter, and protect themselves from Perge's extremely hot summer sun. Because of their suitability for the climate, avenues of this type are frequently found in the cities of southern and western Anatolia. Certainly the most interesting aspect of Perge's collonnaded street is the pool-like water channel that divides the road down the middle. Made to flow by the river god Kestros, these clear, clean waters ran out of a monumental fountain (nymphaeum) at the north end of the street and flowed placidly along the channels, cooling the Pergeians just a little in the cruel Pamphylian heat. At approximately the middle of the street, four relief-carved columns belonging to the portico immediately catch the eye. On the first column, Apollo is depicted riding a chariot drawn by four horses; on the second is Artemis the huntress; the third shows Calchas, one of the city's mythical founders; and the last, Tyche (Fortune).

The main road comes to an end at another nymphaeum built at the foot of the acropolis in the second century A.D. The rich architecture of its twotiered facade and its numerous statues make it one of Perge's most striking monuments. The water brought from the spring empties into a pool beneath the staue of the river god Kestros standing precisely in the centre of the fountain, and from there flows to the streets via channels.

Turning left from the triumphal arch of Apollonios that intersects the streets, and passing the Hellenistic gate, one comes to the palaestra, known to be Perge's oldest building. Here, under the supervision of their teachers, the youth of the city practised wrestling and underwent physical education. According to an inscription this square edifice, consisting of an open area surrounded by rooms, was dedicated to the Emperor Claudius (reigned 41 - 54 A.D.) by a certain C. Julius Cornutus.

Perge, transformed by artisans into a city of marble, was truly magnificent, with a faultless layout that would have been the envy of modern city planners. In order to fully appreciate its grandeur today, one must visit the Antalya Museum to see the hundreds of sculptures from Perge now housed there.

Among the famous men raised in this city can be cited the physician Asklepiades, the sophist Varus, and the mathematician Apollonios.

Perge has been under excavation by Turkish archeologists since 1946.

Capital of a column with Artemis

Mosaics of Perge

Column capital

Column capital

A view of the Agora

SILLYON

This Pamphylian town, located between Perge and Aspendos, is situated on top of a flat-topped hill with almost vertical flanks. With its unusual physical formation, the hill is easily recognizable even from a distance. Strabo mentions in his writings that the city, some 40 stad or 7.2 km, inland, was visible from Perge.

It is generally accepted that Sillyon, like other cities in Pamphylia, was founded after the Trojan War by the heroes Mopsos and Calchas. A statue base found in Sillyon bears Mopsos' name.

Sillyon began to mint coinage in its own name in the third century B.C. On these coins the name of the city was written as Sylviys, which must have been changed to Sillyon in the Roman era.

The name Sillyon is almost never mentioned in history except for its appearance in Arrianos' notes on the campaigns of Alexander the Great. These notes indicate that the reaction of Sillyon's residents to Alexander was hostile, in contrast to that of Perge, and that they defended themselves from a strong position, relying on mercenaries as well as soldiers. In any case it appears that Sillyon had been a military base since Persian times; the remains of buildings and fortifications from the Hellenistic, Roman, Byzantine, and Seljuk epochs reveal that the city preserved its military character for a long time.

Climbing a simple path from Yanköy toward the hill, the first thing one encounters is the lower gate. Consisting of a horseshoe-shaped court with two rectangular towers, it is similar to Perge's Hellenistic gate in its plan and masonry. On this basis it has been dated to the third century B.C.

Because Sillyon is situated on a steep-sided hill, there was no need to surround the city with walls. It was only in the west and southwest sections where the incline is at its slightest, that walls, towers, and ramparts were erected. These exhibit painstaking stonework and considerable technical expertise.

The city's oldest ruins lie north-east of the main entrance gate. The first structure one encounters here is a two-storey, high-walled building from the Byzantine era; although it is in good condition, its function has not yet been ascertained. At the end of it lies one of Sillyon's most important structures, a 7x55 metre palaestra of Hellenistic date. On its west wall are ten windows of differing dimensions. A little further on is a small Helle-

Sillyon

26

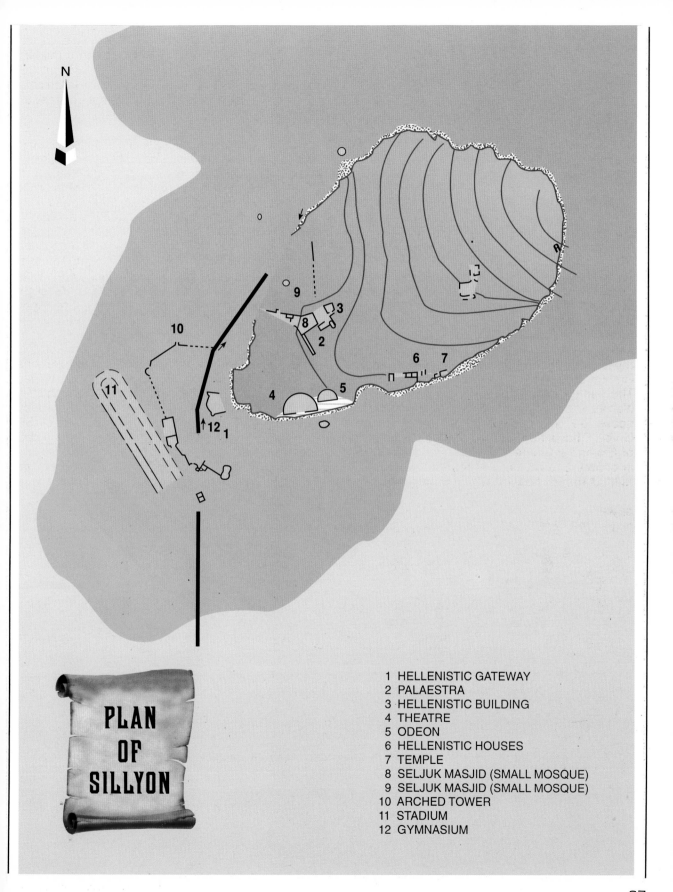

N

R

PLAN
OF
SILLYON

1 HELLENISTIC GATEWAY
2 PALAESTRA
3 HELLENISTIC BUILDING
4 THEATRE
5 ODEON
6 HELLENISTIC HOUSES
7 TEMPLE
8 SELJUK MASJID (SMALL MOSQUE)
9 SELJUK MASJID (SMALL MOSQUE)
10 ARCHED TOWER
11 STADIUM
12 GYMNASIUM

Historical fountain in Sillyon

Remains of the Theatre of Sillyon

nistic building with an elegant door and carefully executed masonry. The building's fame is derived from an inscription, thirty lines in length, is the longest and most important document in this dialect known today. It is a pity that a portion of the inscription was lost when a hole was made in the door at a later date. While the dialect, written in Greek characters, was used in a large part of Pamphylia until the first century A.D., it was gradually forgotten after that date and was replaced by Greek.

At the southern edge of the plateau one encounters a sad scene. The Sillyon theatre and the odeon beside it, described as being in an excellent state of preservation in the 1884 Pamphylian travel notes of the Austrian researcher Lanckoronski, disappeared down the hill in a landslide in 1969; only eleven rows of seats from the cavea were left in place.

Immediately after the theatre, rock-cut stairs with balustrades along the sides lead to Hellenistic houses of square or rectangular plan constructed in the meticulous stonework typical of that period. Going east, one sees a small Hellenistic temple. Rising above a podium measuring 7.30x11.00 metres, the temple's cella wall and stylobate are still standing. According to existing architectural remains, the temple was of the Doric prostyle type.

From the beginning of the thirteenth century the Seljuks settled in Sillyon in small groups, just as they did in certain other cities. In accordance with their custom they built a small, thin-walled, crenelated citadel on the acropolis. The most interesting building that has survived from the Seljuk period is a square, domed mosque in the north-west part of the acropolis.

Other than a few Byzantine and Seljuk buildings there are no important remains at the eastern end of the acropolis. On returning to the village from the upper gate, one passes a necropolis area consisting of simple graves, before arriving at a well preserved tower. Square in plan, the tower has two floors, with a door opening into the lower one. Doors on the upper level placed there for defensive purposes open onto the ramparts. The stadium is on a terrace south-west of the tower. It is in very poor condition; all that remains are the tiers of seats mounted on vaults running along its western length.

There could not have been enough springs in the area to ensure an adequate water supply, since it is clear that importance was given to the construction of covered and open cisterns from the Hellenistic period onward.

29

ASPENDOS

Aspendos, located beside the river Eurymedon (Köprüçay), is renowned throughout the world for its magnificent ancient amphitheatre.

According to Greek legend, the city was founded by Argive colonists who, under the leadership of the hero Mopsos, came to Pamphylia after the Trojan War. Aspendos was one of the first cities in the region to strike coinage under its own name. On these silver staters dated to the fifth and fourth century B.C., however, the name of the city is written as Estwediiys in the local script. A late eighth century B.C. bilingual inscription carved in both Hittite hieroglyphs and the Phoenician alphabet discovered in the 1947 excavation of Karatepe near Adana, states that Asitawada, the king of Danunum (Adana), founded a city called Azitawadda, a derivation of his own name, and that he was a member of the Muksas, or Mopsus, dynasty. The striking similarity between the names 'Estwediiys' and "azitawaddi" suggests the possibility that Aspendos was the city this king founded.

Aspendos did not play an important role in antiquity as a political force. Its political history during the colonization period corresponded to the currents of the Pamphylian region. Within this trend, after the colonial period, it remained for a time under Lycian hegemony. In 546 B.C. it came under Persian domination. The fact that the city continued to mint coins in its own name, however, indicates that it had a great deal of freedom even under the Persians.

In 467 B.C. the statesman and military commander Cimon, and his fleet of 200 ships, destroyed the Persian navy based at the mouth of the river Eurymedon in a surprise attack. In order to crush the Persian land forces, he tricked the Persians by sending his best fighters to shore wearing the garments of the hostages

External facade of the Aspendos Theatre

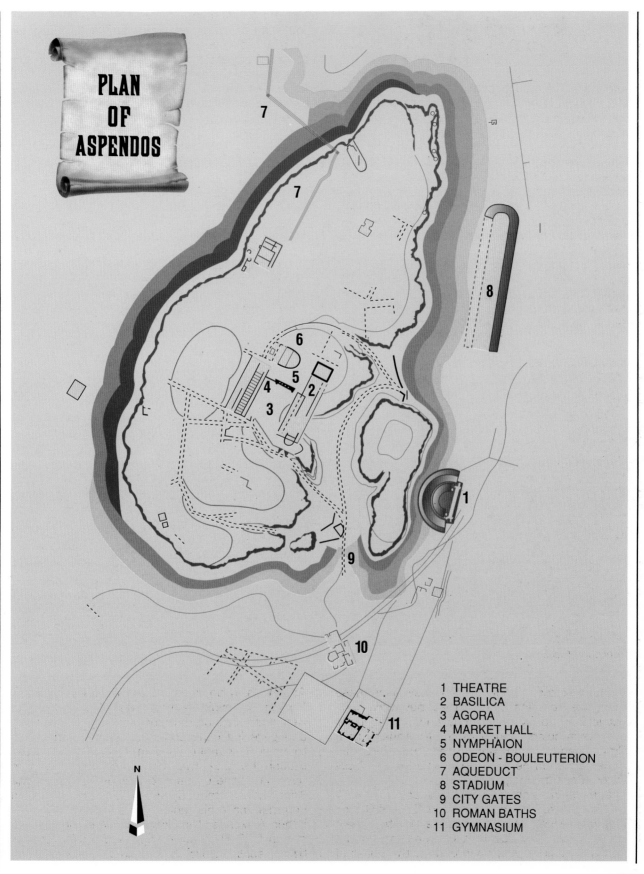

PLAN
OF
ASPENDOS

1 THEATRE
2 BASILICA
3 AGORA
4 MARKET HALL
5 NYMPHAION
6 ODEON - BOULEUTERION
7 AQUEDUCT
8 STADIUM
9 CITY GATES
10 ROMAN BATHS
11 GYMNASIUM

N

Aspendos Theatre

he had seized earlier. When they saw these men, the Persians thought that they were compatriots freed by the enemy and arranged festivities in celebration. Taking advantage of this, Cimon landed and annihilated the Persians. Aspendos then became a member of the Attic-Delos Maritime league.

The Persians captured the city again in 411 B.C. and used it as a base. In 389 B.C. the commander of Athens, in an effort to regain some of the prestige that city had lost in the Peloponnesian Wars, anchored off the coast of Aspendos in an effort to secure its surrender. Hoping to avoid a new war, the people of Aspendos collected money among themselves and gave it to the commander, entreating him to retreat without causing any damage. Even though he took the money, he had his men trample all the crops in the fields. Enraged, the Aspendians stabbed and killed the Athenian commander in his tent.

When Alexander the Great marched into Aspendos in 333 B.C. after capturing Perge, the citizens sent envoys to him to request that he would not establish a garrison in the city. Alexander agreed to their offer on the condition that he be given the taxes and horses that they had formerly paid as tribute to the Persian king. After reaching this agreement, Alexander went to Side, leaving a garrison there on the city's surrender. Going back through Sillyon, he learned that the Aspendians had failed to ratify the agreement their envoys had proposed and were preparing to defend themselves. Alexander marched to the city immediately. When they saw Alexander returning with his troops, the Aspendians, who had retreated to their acropolis, again sent envoys to sue for peace. This time, however, they had to agree to very harsh terms; a Macedonian garrison would remain in the city and 100 gold talents as well as 4,000 horses would be given in tax annually. During the wars that followed the death of Alexander, the city came alternately under the control of the Ptolemies and the Seleucids, later falling into the hands of the Kingdom of Pergamum, to which it remained bound until 133 B.C.

From Cicero's presentation of the case before the Roman senate, we know that in 79 B.C. Gaius Verres, the questor of Cilicia, pillaged Aspendos just as he had Perge. Verres, right in front of the citizens, took statues from the temples and squares and had them loaded into carts. he even had Aspendos' famous statue of a harpist set up in his own home.

Aspendos, like most of the other Pamphylian cities, reached its height in the second and third centuries A.D. Most of the monumental architecture still visible here today dates to this golden age. Although the city was not on the coast, the river Eurymedon, on whose banks it was situated, allowed ships to reach it. This accessibility, together with the productive plain

Stage of the Aspendos Theatre

Inside of the Aspendos Theatre

and the thickly forested mountains that lay behind Aspendos, were major factors in its development. Gold and silver embroidered tapestries woven in the city, furniture and figurines made from the wood of lemon trees, salt obtained from nearby Lake Capria, wine, and especially the famous horses of Aspendos were its foremost exports. Although they were renowned as grape growers and wine merchants, they did not offer wine to their gods in their religious rites. They explained this omission by saying that if wine were reserved for the gods, birds would not have the courage to eat grapes.

Few Aspendians made a name for themselves in history. Andromachos was a famous military commander in his day and was also the governor of Phoenicia and Syria. Little is known of the work of the native philosopher Diodorus, but that he wore the long hair, dirty clothes, and bare feet of the Cynics, which suggests he was influenced by Pythagorus.

At the beginning of the thirteenth century, Aspendos began to bear the imprint of settlement by the Seljuk Turks, especially during the reign of Alaeddin Keykubat I. when the theatre

The arches of the Theatre

Reconstruction of the skene of the Aspendos Theatre

Aspendos coins, 3rd-4th centuries A.D.

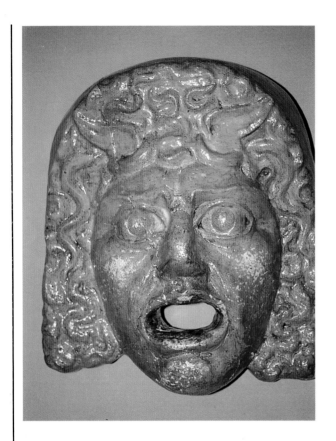

Imitations of the theatre masks

Basilica

Aerial view of Basilica and the city

was thoroughly restored, embellished in Seljuk style with elegant tiles, and used as a palace.

At the end of the road that turns off the Antalya-Alanya highway, we come to the most magnificent, as well as functionally the best resolved and most complete example of a Roman theatre. The building, faithful to the Greek tradition, is partially built into the slope of a hill. Today visitors enter the stage building via a door opened in the facade during a much later period. The original entrances, however, are the vaulted paradoses at both ends of the stage building. The cavea is semicircular in shape and divided in two by a large diazoma. There are 21 tiers of seats above and 20 below. To provide ease of circulation so that the spectators could reach their seats without difficulty, radiating stairways were built, 10 in the lower level starting at the orchestra and 21 in the upper beginning at the diazoma. A wide gallery consisting of 59 arches and thought to have been built at a later date, goes from one end of the upper cavea to the other. From an architectural point of view, the diazoma's vaulted gallery acts

The antique Aspendos Bridge

The Aquaducts of Aspendos

Aspendos Theatre

as a substructure supporting the upper cavea. As a general rule of protocol, the private boxes above the entrances on both sides of the cavea were reserved for the Imperial family and the vestal virgins. Beginning from the orchestra and going up, the first row of seats belonged to senators, judges, and ambassadors, while the second was reserved for other notables of the city. The remaining sections were open to all the citizens. The women usually sat on the upper rows under the gallery. From the names carved on certain seats in the upper cavea, it is clear that these too were reserved. Although it is impossible to determine the exact seating capacity of the theatre, it is said to have seated between 10,000 and 12,000 people. In recent years, concerts given in the theatre, as part of the Antalya Film and Art Festival, have shown that as many as 20,000 spectators can be crowded into the seating area.

Without doubt the Aspendos theatre's most striking component is the stage building. On the lower floor of this two-storey structure, which is built of conglomerate rock, were five doors providing the actors entrance to the stage. The large door at the centre was known as the porta regia, and the two smaller ones on either side as the porta hospitales. The small doors at orchestra level belong to long corridors leading to the areas where the wild animals were kept. From surviving fragments it appears that sculptural works were placed in niches and aedicula under triangular and semicircular pediments.

In the pediment at the centre of the colonnaded upper floor is a relief of Dionysos, the god of wine and the founder and patron of theatres. Red zigzag motifs against white plaster, visible on some portions of the stage building, date to the Seljuk period. The top of the stage building is covered with a highly ornamented wooden roof.

The theatre at Aspendos is also famous for its magnificent accoustics. Even the sligtest sound made at the centre of the orchestra can be easily heard as far as the uppermost galleries.

Anatolia's patricians, who lived in the midst of a rich cultural heritage, created stories connected with the cities and monuments around them. One of these tales which has been passed down from generation to generation is about Aspendos' theatre. The king of Aspendos proclaimed that he would hold a contest to see what man could render the greatest service to the city; the winner would marry the king's daughter. Hearing this, the artisans of the city began to work at high speed. At last, when the day of the decision came and the king had exa-

mined all their efforts one by one, he designated two candidates. The first of them had succeeded in setting up a system that enabled water to be brought to the city from great distances via aqueducts. The second built the theatre. Just as the king was on the point of deciding in favour of the first candidate, he was asked to have one more look at the theatre. While he was wandering about in the upper galleries, a deep voice from an unknown source rang out saying again and again, "The king's daughter must be given to me". In asto-

Aerial view of the Aspendos Theatre

nishment the king looked around for the owner of the voice but could find no one. It was, of course, the architect himself, proud of the accoustical masterpiece he had created, who was speaking in a low voice from the stage. In the end, it was the architect who won the beautiful girl and the wedding ceremony took place in the theatre.

We know from an inscription in the southern parados that the theatre was constructed during the reign of the Emperor Marcus Aurelieus (161-180 A.D.) by the architect Zeno, the son of an Aspendian named Theoduros. According to the inscription, the people of Aspendos, out of admiration for Zeno, awarded him a large garden beside the stadium. Greek and Latin inscriptions above the entrances on both sides of the stage building tell us that, two brothers named Curtius Crispinus and Curtius Auspicatus commissioned the building and dedicated it to the gods and the Imperial family.

No fee was charged for putting on a performance in the theatre. A portion of the necessary production costs were covered by civic institutions, but after the performance, part of the profits was turned over to these organizations. Generally one had to pay a fee or buy tickets to gain entry to plays or competitions. Tickets were made of metal, ivory, bone, or in most cases, fired clay, with a picture on one side and a row and seat number on the other.

Aspendos' other principal remains are above the acropolis, behind the theatre. The first building one comes to on the acropolis, which is reached via a footpath starting alongside the theatre, is a basilica measuring 27x105 metres. The basilica is an architectural form invented by the Romans. Roman basilicas were used for a wide variety of purposes, but these were all concerned with public affairs. Markets and law courts were set up in buildings. The basilica plan consists of a large central hall surrounded by smaller chambers. The central hall is separated from those at the sides by co-

The Aquaducts of Aspendos

Aquaducts of the city

lumns and its roof is higher. Inside the basilica is a tribunal. During the Byzantine era the building underwent major alterations and lost much of its original character.

South of the basilica and bounded on three sides by houses, is the agora, the centre of the city's commercial, social, and political activities. A little further to the west are twelve shops of equal size all in a line at the rear of a stoa.

North of the agora is a nymphaeum of which only the front wall remains standing. Measuring 32.5 m. in width by 15 m. in height, this two-level facade has five niches at each level. The middle niche in the lower level is larger than the others and is thought to have been used as a door. It is clear from the marble bases at the foot of the wall that the building originally had a colonnaded facade.

Behind the nymphaeum is a building of unusual plan, either an odeon or a bouleuterion where council members met.

Another of Aspendos' remains that should not be missed is its aqueduct. This one kilometre-long series of arches which brought water to the city from mountains at the north, represents an extraordinary feat of engineering and is one of the rare examples surviving from antiquity. The water was brought from is source in a channel formed by hollowed stone blocks on top of 15 metre-high arches. Near both ends of the aqueduct the water was collected in towers some 30 metres high, which was distributed to the city.

An inscription found in Aspendos tells us that a certain Tiberius Claudius Italicus had the aqueduct built, and presented it to the city. Its architectural features and construction techniques date it to the middle of the second century A.D.

Antique Remains

Antique Remains

Basilica and Monumental fountain (Nymphaeum)

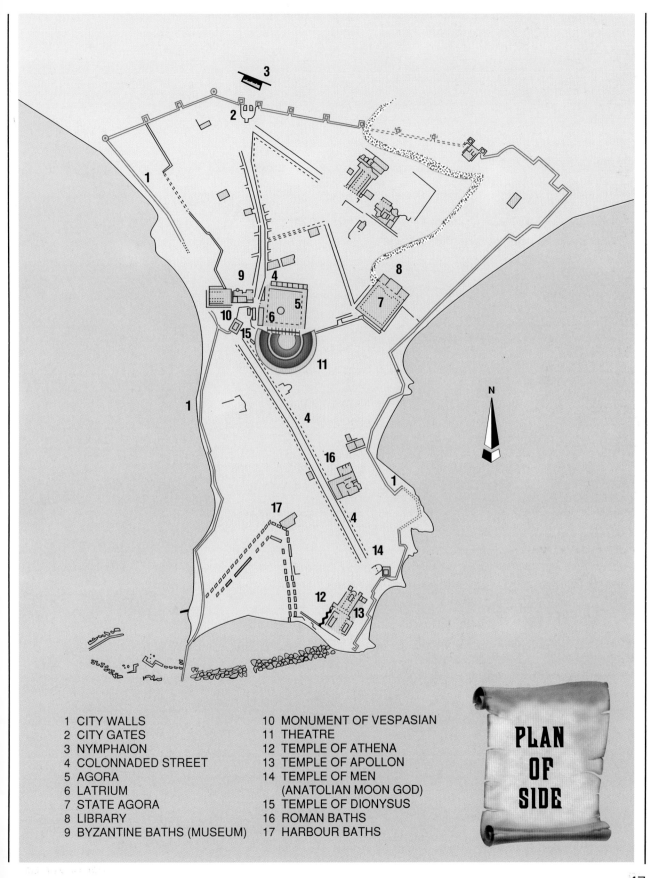

1 CITY WALLS
2 CITY GATES
3 NYMPHAION
4 COLONNADED STREET
5 AGORA
6 LATRIUM
7 STATE AGORA
8 LIBRARY
9 BYZANTINE BATHS (MUSEUM)
10 MONUMENT OF VESPASIAN
11 THEATRE
12 TEMPLE OF ATHENA
13 TEMPLE OF APOLLON
14 TEMPLE OF MEN
   (ANATOLIAN MOON GOD)
15 TEMPLE OF DIONYSUS
16 ROMAN BATHS
17 HARBOUR BATHS

PLAN OF SIDE

Aerial view of Side

SIDE

Side, ancient Pamphylia's largest port, is situated on a small peninsula extending north-south into the sea.

Strabo and Arrianos both record that Side was settled from Kyme, city in Aeolia, a region of western Anatolia. Most probably, this colonization occurred in the seventh century B.C. According to Arrianos, when settlers from Kyme came to Side, they could not understand the dialect. After a short while, the influence of this indigenous tongue was so great that the newcomers forgot their native Greek and started using the language of Side. Excavations have revealed several inscriptions written in this language. The inscriptions, dating from the third and second centuries B.C., remain undeciphered, but testify that the local language was still in use several centuries after colonization. Another object found in Side excavations, a basalt column base from the seventh century B.C. and attributable to the Neo Hittites, provides other evidence of the site's early history. The word "side" is Anatolian in origin and means pomegranate.

No information exists concerning Side under Lydian and Persian sovereignty. Nevertheless, the fact that Side minted its own coins during the fifth century B.C. while under Persian dominion, shows that it still possessed a great measure of independence.

In 333 B.C., despite its strong land and sea walls, Side surrendered to Alexander the Great without a fight.

For a long period following the death of Alexander, Side came under the dominion of the Ptolemaic and Seleucid Empires, and in 190 B.C. witnessed a great naval battle. This encounter took place between the fleet of Rhodes, acting with the support of Rome and Pergamum, and the fleet of Antiochos III, the king of Syria, under the command of the famous Carthaginian Hannibal. Side took the side of Hannibal, but the Rhodian forces carried the day.

In the second century B.C. Side was able to stave off the forces of the Attaleids of Pergamum and preserve its independence, becoming a wealthy commercial, intellectual, and entertainment centre. Side's importance in the Eastern Mediterranean as an educational and cultural centre can be gauged by the fact that Antiochos VII, who ascended the throne of Syria in 138 B.C., was sent to Side in his youth to receive his education.

In the first century B.C. misfortune overtook Side in the form of Cilician pirates, who seized the city and turned it into a naval base and slave market. The people of Side seem to have tolerated the pirates because of the highly profitable nature of this commerce, which, however, gave the city a bad name in the region. Stratonicus, a man famous for his retorts and witticisms, answered the question, "Who are the worst, most treacherous people?" saying, "In Pamphylia the people of Phaselis, but in the whole world the people of Side". The famous Roman general Pompey ended the reign of the pirates in 7 B.C., and Side, by erecting monuments and statues in his honour, tried to erase its bad name.

Under Roman rule, Side prospered during a second golden age, especially in the second and third centuries when it became a metropolis, seat of the provincial governor and his administrative staff. Due to its large harbour, Side in this era enjoyed commercial relations

Fountain of Vespasian

External facade of the theatre

General view of Side

General view of the Cleopatra Beach

throughout the Mediterranean particularly with Egypt. Imported goods left Side for central Anatolia by road. Side's importance as a commercial centre can be ascertained by the hundreds of shops occupying not only the main streets, but also the narrowest of side streets and alleys. At the same time it continued as an important slave trading centre. Documents from the Imperial Roman period found in Egypt report that these slaves were sent to Side mainly from Africa. It is also known that Side possessed a large commercial fleet which did not pass up opportunities to commit piracy. Maritime commerce was the origin of the wealth of many merchants. These wealthy men did not work solely to increase their fortunes, but also provided for activities benefiting the people of the city, donating large sums to organize competitions and games, as well as to beautify the city and create social and religious organizations. One inscription found above a late period gate reports that two people, whose names cannot be made out, had a deipnisterion or soup kitchen erected for the use of government employees and the council of elders. A woman named Modesta organized gladiatorial events; Tuesianos, another inhabitant of Side, organized a feast to celebrate the return of the seamen to Side; and a husband and wife pair of philanthropists provided for the repairs of Side's water system out of their own pockets. A great proportion of the buildings and monuments still standing at Side date to this magnificent epoch.

Side's last years of plenty occurred in the fifth and sixth centuries A.D. when it served as the seat of the Bishopric of Eastern Pamphylia. At this time there was much construction, and the city expanded beyond the extant city walls.

Starting in the middle of the seventh century, destructive raids by Arab fleets on the southern coast of Anatolia transformed it into a war zone. Side was naturally, affected, and excavations have uncovered ashy burnt layers showing that the city was entirely burnt by the Arabs.

According to the twelfth century Arab geographer Idrisi, Side was at one time a large and populous city, but after being sacked it was abandoned by its inhabitants, who moved to An-

The Apollo Temple at Sunset

talya, two days' journey away; as a result, according to Idrisi, Side became known as Old Antalya.

In order to protect itself from threats coming by land or sea, Side was surrounded on all four sides by high walls. The sea walls have been much altered over the centuries due to repair and rebuilding and have lost much of their original appearance; they have even collapsed in several places. By contrast, the land walls and their towers are almost whole, due to their having been carefully constructed of conglomerate stone. The city is entered through two gates in the eastern fortification wall. The large main gate was built during the Hellenistic period. It is flanked by two towers and gives onto a horseshoe-shaped courtyard. After passing through the courtyard and a square room, one enters the city. As is the case in Perge, the gate and courtyard complex were ornamented with many storeys of columns in the second century A.D. and transformed into a ceremonial place of honour. The second largest city gate, also belonging to the Hellenistic period, lies on the north-east of the city; behind its square towers lies a courtyard that is also square in form.

The main street starts from this north-eastern gate and stretches all the way to the peninsula's western tip in an almost completely straight line. Along this street lay the city's

principal official buildings and its squares. Excavations have revealed a perfectly planned sewer system. This system, covered with vaults, lay under the main street as well as the smaller streets.

Outside the city wall and opposite the main gate lies the nymphaeum, a monumental fountain consisting of richly ornamented facade with three niches and with a fountain in front. Piped-in water used to flow from spouts in the middle of these niches.

The agora, the city's centre of commercial and cultural activity, lay along an arcaded street. It can be entered today from immediately opposite the museum. This square space was surrounded on all four sides by porticoes. Rows of stores can still be observed running behind the north-east and north-west porticoes. An interesting vaulted building lies in the agora's south-west corner adjacent to the theatre, this served as the city's latrium or public toilets and is the most highly ornamented and best preserved example in Anatolia. Sewers carried away the waste from this establishment, which had a 24-toilet capacity, while in front of the building ran a channel carrying only purified water.

In the middle of the agora lay a circular temple dedicated to Tyche (Fortune). All that is left today is the podium of this structure, but originally twelve columns ran around its exterior and the temple was topped by a pyramidal roof.

This agora was linked to a second, state agora by a street running along its southern edge. This agora, too, was square in plan and was enclosed by porticoes of Ionic columns. It is believed that the high platform in the middle of the agora was used for the display and sale of slaves. Behind the eastern portico lay a large ornamented three-chambered building which, due to its architectural peculiarities, is thought to have been either an imperial palace or a library. From extant remains it can be ascertained that the building was originally two storeys and richly adorned with statues. Aside from a statue of Nemesis, which has been left in place to recall the original decorative style, all the statues found during excavation have been removed to the Side Museum.

The agora bathhouse, today used as the museum, is a five-room Byzantine structure dating to the fifth century A.D. It is entered through two arched doorways. The first room, possessing a small cold water pool, was the frigidarium. From here one passes to a stone-domed sweating room or loconicum. The third and largest of the structure's rooms is the hot room or caldarium. The bath's heating system ran beneath the marble flooring. From the caldarium one can enter the two-room tepidarium or washing area through a narrow door. In front of the bath was a palaestra with a porticoed courtyard where men could excercise before bathing.

Next to the triumphal arch, which at a late date was used a city gate, lies a beautiful monument, partially restored in recent years. This monument consists of a niche between two aedicules and, according to an inscription found in the architrave, was built in 74 A.D. in memory of the Emperor Vespasian and his son Titus. During the construction of the late period city wall in the fourth century A.D., this monument was brought here from elsewhere in the city and turned into a fountain.

The theatre is the only extant example of its plan and construction type to be found in Anatolia. It was erected in the second century A.D. on Hellenistic foundations. Because Side is virtually flat, the theatre's lower banks had to be built into the only natural rise available, which is not very steep, while the upper banks of seats overlay an arched substructure. Twenty nine seating levels can be counted below the 3.30 metre-wide diazoma, which divides the cavea in two. In the upper section only twenty

Sunset from the antique harbour of Side

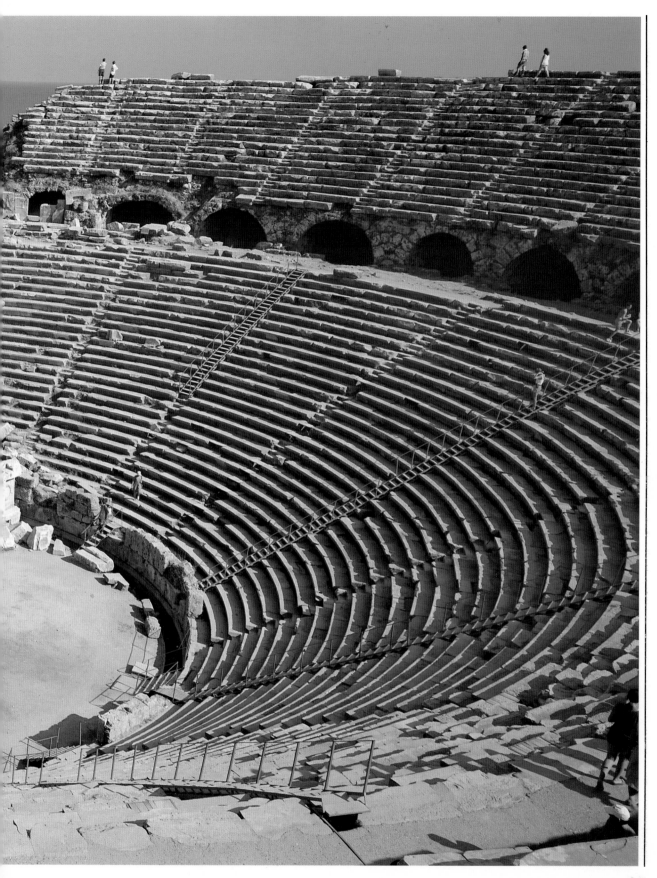

Side by night

two of the original twenty nine rows survive. Thus, this was Pamphylia's largest theatre and had a seating capacity of 16-17,000 people. In the outside gallery of the lower section, staircases rose to the diazoma. From interior galleries, staircases ascended to the theatre's upper section. The galleries' two ends probably contained paradoses, enabling them to be used as entrances for theatre staff and actors.

The orchestra was slightly larger than a semicircle, and at a late date it was surrounded by a high thick wall that rendered inoperative the lowest banks of seats. This wall was covered with waterproof pink plaster which allowed

Shops in Side

The Apollo Temple by night

Theatre

Agora

the orchestra to be filled from time to time with water for reenactments of naval battles and other sports; it no doubt also served as a pit for displays of wild animal combat. These displays usually pitted predatory animals against one another or against gladiators. Sometimes even unarmed people-criminals, slaves, and prisoners-were set against wild animals, and their helpless struggle was followed with rude glee.

A stage building rose off a wide podium behind the orchestra. It consisted of a two-storey facade 63 metres in length. On the podium, five narrow doors linked the orchestra ornamented with coloumns, niches and statues, and its lower storey contained five large openings allowing for the actors, and its entrance. Between these openings, just as in the theatre at Perge, were marble friezes illustrating Dionysiac themes. The stage building's reliefs have been transported to the agora for the duration of the restoration work which has newly begun in this area.

During the troubles of the fourth century A.D., a new fortification wall was built, and this wall took advantage of the high back wall of the stage building. During the fifth and sixth cen-

The Apollo Temple

turies A.D., the theatre was used as an open-air church, and the parados sections were decorated with floor mosaics and transformed into small chapels.

The most varied and beautiful temples in all of Pamphylia are to be found in Side. Two stupendous temples rose on the peninsula's southern point, right next to each other, the sea and the harbour. These temples were built in the second half of the second century A.D. Consisting entirely of marble, they are of the peripteros type and employ the Corinthian

The large beach and the hotels of Side

A view of Side

Dough cooking women

The Apollo Temple

The beach of Side

order. The short sides have six columns each, the long sides eleven. In the fifth century A.D. a large basilica was built in front of these temples, incorporating them into its atrium. Despite being heavily damaged, the temples' ancient configuration can be determined. Because Side's patron goddess was Athena, it is highly probable that one of the temples was dedicated to Athena, who in consequence, would have been featured extremely prominently as a protectress of the harbour and of sailors. As for the other temple, it must have been dedicated to Apollo. Restoration of the Temple of Apollo is ongoing.

Further on, to the east of the last big square off the arcaded street, lies a semicircular temple dedicated to the god Men. The cella of this temple was entered from the west by a staircase up the high podium. At the top of the stairs are four Corinthian columns. This temple dates to the end of the second century A.D.

Between the arcaded street and the theatre lie the remains of an early Roman temple. Of this temple, which is of the pseudo-peripteral type, only the podium remains. The podium is ascended from the north by seven steps. In front of the cella rise four granite Corinthian columns. Because of its proximity to the theatre, it is thought that this temple belonged to Dionysos.

Dating to the third century A.D., the biggest of Side's three public baths lies on the arcaded street. Its dimensions are 40x50 metres and it is a beautiful building in a fine state of preservation. Its various rooms are vaulted. The broad courtyard in front of this building was most likely used as a palaestra.

In order to satisfy their desire for a plentiful water supply, the people of Side went to almost superhuman lengths. Water from the head of the Melas river (today's Manavgat Çayı) reached Side after an adventure some 30 kilometre journey on two-storeyed arched aqueducts, passing through channels carved out of cliffs, and vaulted tunnels and across valleys before it was collected in city cisterns, from which it was distrubuted in clay pipes.

Large cemeteries lie outside the city wall. In these cemeteries one can still see many types of graves, be they simple square holes, plain or carved sarcophagi, or magnificent memorials in the form of temples. These areas were called necropoli, cities of the dead. The most beautiful of these can be found in the western cemetery near the sea. On a podium reached by stairs rises a building shaped like a temple with four columns. Inside this building, marble sarcophagi are situated in arched niches. This building dates to the second century A.D., and together with its ornamented courtyard must have served as the tomb of a wealthy family.

Side has been excavated by Turkish archeologists since 1947, and excavations continue intermiltently.

Monumental library

SIDE MUSEUM

The Side Museum occupies the ancient city's agora bathhouse which was constructed in the fifth century B.C. The structure was excavated by Turkish archeologists between 1955 and 1961, restored, and turned into the present museum, being opened to visitors in 1961.

The grounds of the museum are entered by passing along an ancient road near the walls of Philippus Attius. In antiquity the five chambers making up the hamam were vaulted; only three of these were covered in the course of restoration. Originally a door opening from the palaestra to the frigidarium gave entry to the bath. Today, however, one enters the museum from the te-

pidarium. A large statue of a nike stands before the common wall separating this room, which usually exhibits inscriptions uncovered in the Side excavations, from the frigidarium. The statue portray this winged goddess symbolizing victory at the moment she is gliding from the heavens to alight on earth. Beneath her feet are spoils of war seized from the enemy. This work dates to the second century A.D.

Now the first gallery, the frigidarium, with its round, cold water pool, was once the bath's cooling room. The basalt column base at the centre of the gallery is the oldest object so far recovered from Side. The base, which dates to the Neo-Hittite period (seventh century B.C.) was found near the temple of Athena. In all probability a Sidetan merchant who went to south-east Anatolia

The Side Museum

Hermes, 2 nd century A.D.

brought it back with him and presented it to the temple.

Reliefs showing spoils that Side won in a war fought in the second century B.C. are exhibited on the wall across from the cold water pool.

The caldarium, which contains five pools, forms the largest gallery. The works exhibited here have been placed in niches beside the pools. Statues of clothed females from the Hellenistic period stand in the two niches of the big pool the left of the door that leads to the loconium. In the niche to the left of the two semicircular pools is a section of an interesting relief dating to the second century B.C. and illustrating the punishment of Ixion. When Ixion was about to marry, his prospective father-in-law asked for gifts. The youth responded by promising that he would bring presents only in the event that he was given permission to marry the girl. He did not keep his word after the wedding, however, and his relationship with his father-in-law went sour. Ixion then invited the old man to his house for dinner under the pretext that he wanted to make peace and present his father-in-law with the gifts. Instead, the poor man was taken from the banquet table, to which he had come with such high hopes, and thrown alive into a flaming pit where he burned to death. This detestable murder was repugnant to both the people and the gods, and no one would forgive Ixion. Somehow, however, this man, though despised by everyone, managed to ingratiate himself with Zeus, the king of the gods, and obtain pardon for his crime. Not stopping there, he even managed to get himself invited to dine with the gods, but at the table, the treacherous murderer, betraying Zeus' clemency, looked at Zeus' wife, the virtuous Hera, with a lustful eye and even declared his love to her. Enraged at these goings on, Zeus formed a bit of cloud into an image of Hera and sent it near Ixion. By now, thoroughly drunk on nectar, the wine of immortality, Ixion threw his arms out to embrace the apparition. Seeing this, Zeus bound the ungreatful youth to a burning wheel and condemned him to eternal torment. As the wheel continues to turn, Ixion, the murderer and enemy of virtue, continues to burn.

Also beside the pool containing the Ixion relief, is a statue of the river god who personifies the Melas river (Manavgat Irmağı), In antiquity the river and streams that gave cities life were also considered to be gods and were generally depicted as reclining males. The water pouring from a vessel under his arm symbolizes the turbulent flow of the Melas.

The statue of Heracles at the centre of the gallery represents him in one of the twelve difficult and

Punishment of Ixion, 2 nd century A.D.

Three Beauties, 3 rd century A.D.

dangerous labours that the hero managed to carry out. Heracles was ordered to find the Garden of the Hespedires, which was in an unknown country and which contained valuable trees on which golden apples grew. He was to pick these apples and bring them back. Heracles, with his great strength, found the way and arrived at the garden gate. There, at the end of the earth, was a giant named Atlas, who had been given the punishment of having to hold up the world on his tireless arms and head. Heracles asked Atlas what had to be done in order to obtain the golden apples. The poor giant, who had taken the weight of the earth on his shoulders, asked Heracles to carry the earth himself until he, Atlas, could get the apples and return. The hero agreed and took the world on his shoulders. When Atlas came back, he said that he would take the golden apples himself. The giant's trick annoyed Heracles, but he didn't let it show and appeared to agree to the suggestion. "I want you to take the apples yourself, but before you set out, take the world back for a little bit while I go and get a pillow to put on top of my head", he said. Atlas, without suspecting anything, took the world back on his own shoulders. As soon as Heracles had escaped from the heavy burden, he grabbed the apples and ran to his master. Hence, in this statue, the hero is shown with apples hidden behind him. The work dates to the second cen-

tury A.D.

Across from the door leading to the tepidarium is a statuary group of the three Graces, a frequent subject in art from the Hellenistic period onwards. This particular example dates to the second century A.D. and was unearthed in the excavation of the theatre.

From the caldarium, a narrow, door leads to the section where the bathing proper took place, the tepidarium. The most outstanding sculptural works in the museum's collections are exhibited in this gallery. The superb marble Hermes head, found in the fountain beside the museum, dates to the second century A.D. When one looks carefully at the work, however, one realizes that two pieces along the top were added to the sculpture during a later period. Toward the end of the third century A.D., perhaps because it was needed elsewhere, Hermes most distinctive feature, his winged cap or petasos, was broken off; as a result, the sculpture for many years was thought to represent the god Apollo.

In the last niche in the room is a statue of an emperor, interesting in that it is another example reflecting two different periods. The emperor's armour - clad body can be dated to the second century A.D. on the basis of its stylistic features. The head, however, exhibits fourth century characteristics and is much too small for the body. From the middle of the second century A.D. for

Statue of an emperor, body: 2 nd century A.D., head: 3 rd century A.D.

Statue of Heracles, 2 nd century A.D.

example, hair and beards were shown as long, coarse and loosely curling, while in the fourth century, in keeping with the fashion of the day, the curls were chipped and carved off and and transformed into hair and beards defined with simple chisel strokes. In the late Roman Empire, easy procedures .of this sort were frequently resorted to as a means of saving time and money in the making of statues of the frequently changing emperors. Without altering the body of a perivous emperor's statue, either the new emperor's portrait head was mounted on it, or, as the example here, the original head was reworked.

The first statue in the left row at the central section of the gallery is a beautiful second century A.D. copy of the famous fifth century B.C. work known as the Discus Thrower. The athlete is depicted just as he coils his body for the throw.

One of the unique works in the museum is a statue of Hermes in the row on the right. The protector of thieves, merchants and borders, the messenger god holds a bag of money in his right hand. To the left of this is a support bearing a carved representation of male genitals and a be-

Piece of a Sarcophagus, 3 rd century A.D.

A frieze with eagle

Birth of Aphrodite, 2 nd century A.D.

Eros Sarcophagus of Pamphylia, 3 rd century A.D.

arded head. This type of support was know as a Herme and in this case supported the statue of Hermes. The work dates to the second century A.D.

Two sarcophagi and a circular altar occupy the open area at the centre of the gallery. The second century B.C. sarcophagus at the front is of the Attic type. A male figure reclines on the lid, which is shaped like a couch. Three sides of the sarcophagus body are given over to a festive crowd of plump children amusing themselves and playing a variety of musical instruments. The scene ends on one of the narrow ends with a depiction of a sacrifice. Two coarsely carved griffons occupy the fourth side of the sarcophagus, the back.

Garland-carrying Eroses are portrayed on all four sides of the second sarcophagus, this is one of the Pamphylian type. At the corners are winged Nikes holding palm fronds. On one of the pediments, in the form of a rounded roof, is a Medusa's head, and on the other a shield. Found in Side's east mausoleum, the sarcophagus dates to the late second century A.D.

The palaestra and market sections of the bath are used today as the Museum's garden. Here sarcophagi, ossuaries, and architectural fragments are generally on exhibit.

Mosaic of Orpheus

SELEUKIA (PAMPHYLIA)

Situated 23 km to the north-east of Side and near the village of Sihlar, is Seleukia, once a city of Pamphylia. Travelling there from Side, you see an aqueduct which once carried Side's water supply to that city. The ancient city of Selekia was protected by sheer cliffs to the north, east and west. A wall on its southern boundary gave protection on that side; a gate flanked by two towers, opened into the city. Opposite, stood the Roman agora, which was surrounded by shopping galleries in the Doric order. Two-storeyed originally, far more of the lower storey remains, as the upper storey was built of wood. Four main entrances opened into the agora, and from its northern stoa, the floor mosaic of Orpheus, which was once there, has been removed and is now exhibited in the museum at Antalya.

South-east and next to the agora stood the palace, a semicircular building with four main doors. North of the agora was the heroon, with a podium and façade of four columns. West of the city is the bath, one wall of the bath is virtually complete today. Several other remains are on this site, but it is not always easy to tell what

Statue of Apollo (Bronze, 2 nd century A.D.)

they once were. Decorative elements found on the site have been taken to the museum in Antalya; they include a bronze statue of Apollo, a head of Asklepios, the Orpheus mosaic mentioned before, and a figure of Leto.

MANAVGAT WATERFALLS

Manavgat is another of the lovely riverside beauty spots to be found in this region. The 5 m high falls are not as high as those at Düden, but they are spectacular in the volume of water pouring over them. This is a perfect place to sit at one of the little restaurants, and eat fresh trout from the river (for which it is famous) under shady trees. Manavgat is 70 km from Alanya and 80 km from Antalya.

General view of Manavgat

Manavgat River

Manavgat Waterfalls

SELGE

Selge was an important Pisidian city. It lies on the southern slopes of the Taurus in a naturally fortified spot difficult of access. It is reached by a forest road that climbs past cliffs, rivers, and small waterfalls, then passes over a Roman bridge. Thanks to its natural and historical treasures, it has been included in the Köprülü kanyon (Bridged Canyon) National Park.

According to Strabo, Selge's founder was Calchas, and it was later resettled by the Lacedaemonies (Spartans). The first settlement occurred during the Doric migrations which took place at the end of the second millennium B.C. and were connected with the Trojan War. The second settlement took place at the beginning of the seventh century B.C. together with the colonization of Rhodes. No inscription confirming this has come to light in the city, however, and the idea that colonists would choose a place hard to spot from the coast and hidden in the mountains seems difficult to accept.

Selge was the first Pisidian city to mint coins. The silver staters minted in Selge starting in the fifth century B.C. conformed to Persian standards and exhibit a startlingly close resemblance to the coins of Aspendos, from which it is hard to differentiate them. On the obverse of these coins are two wrestlers; on the reverse appear a figure using a slingshot and the city's name, written as Stlegiys or Estlegiys. These local names are linguistic proof that the Pisidian language, which was related to Luvian, a language we know to have been

Selge Theatre

spoken in third millenium Pisidia, was still in use in the fifth century B.C.

We do not possess any continuous account of the city's history. According to the sources, Selge, an ancient foe of Termessos, took up sides with Alexander the Great when he came here. Most likely Selge was at war with its neighbours almost all the time, due to the deep-seated and widespread tendency to bellicosity in this region. We learn of an interesting event connected with Selge, from Polybius. In 218 B.C. Selge and Pednellissos, another Pisidian city, were at war. Selge had a large population and was capable of fielding about 20,000 soldiers. At this time many Pisidian cities were allied to Selge, and so they besieged Pednelissos. The people of Pednelissos appealed to Achaios, uncle of Antiochos III, king of Syria, for help, and he gave the task of lifting the siege to Garsyeris, one of his generals. Polybios relates the rest of the incident as follows.

The people of Pednelissos appealed to Achaios for assistance. He in turn sent the trusted Garsyeris and 6,500 men as help. However, the people of Selge prevented Garsyeris' arrival by seizing the main passes and cutting off access to them. While marching from Millias to Kretopolis, Garsyeris heard the news that the passes had been closed, and he turned home. The people of Selge too pulled back, returned to their houses and started the harvest. However, this was a ruse, because Garsyeris immediately returned, seized the pass of Kretopolis and, stationing a force there, moved into Pamphylia, entering into contact with the enemies of Selge at Perge. He received pledges of assistance from them. In the meantime the troops of Selge tried to recapture the pass held by Garsyeris' men, but they were unsuccessful. They continued to wage war against Pednellissos and did not lift the siege. Because Pednellissos was suffering from starvation. Garsyeris decided to try to smuggle 200 men into the town, each laden with a bag of wheat. However, this attempt was unsuccessful and everything fell into the hands of the Selgeans. Bolstered by their own success. Selge's troops took the offensive and attacked. Leaving only a small force around Pednelissos, they threw their full force against Garsyeris and soon thereafter had him pressed into a very tight corner. Garsyeris counterattacked the enemy's rear with his cavalry in a surprise raid and was victorious. At the same time the people of Pednelissos were freed, and they attacked what remained of the enemy. The Selgeans suffered a heavy loss of some 10,000 men. The remaining troops escaped to the city, but Garsyeris would give them no chance. He immediately followed them, sealing the passes, and appeared outside Selge. Their spirit broken and suing for peace, the people of Selge sent out one of their leading citizens, Logbasis, as an envoy, but Logbasis, betraying the trust of his fellow citizens delivered Selge to Garsyeris, who immediately occupied the city. Garsyeris extended peace negotiations until the arrival of Achaios. When Achaios reached the city, using a trick devised by Logbasis, he called the citizens and guards to a meeting. While the citizens were in the meeting, Achaios, with Logbasis help, was just about to seize Selge and the Temple of Zeus at the Kesbedion outside the city, when the trick failed. A shepherd saw the troops and spread alarm. The Selgeans gathered just in time. First they attacked Logbasis' house, killing him, his sons, and all his men, then they rushed to the defence of the city. they even freed all the slaves. Achaios was driven out at great loss of life. Immediately following this, the Selgeans appealed to Achaios to come to terms, and so they made peace, with the proviso that Selge pay an initial amount of 400 talents, and subsequently 300 talents more, and that it free all the prisoners taken from Pednelissos. The Selgeans thus regained their lands and their freedom.

As can be seen, the people of Selge kept their freedom but had to pay a heavy price for it. That they were able to pay is proof of the city's prosperity.

Strabo praises the city's natural beauties, its fruitful orchards, its wide pastures and forests. He also reports that the inhabitants of Selge often travelled great distances. The main source of revenue for the city was its production of olives, wine, and medicinal plants.

With the founding of the Kingdom of Galatia in 25 B.C., Selge lost its independence for a time. However, under Roman rule, Selge enjoyed good relations. Right up until the breakup of the empire, it kept its independent status and would not concede its beloved lands to anyone. We also know by the frequent minting of coins until the third century that the city's economic life remained healthy. The Goths, who were settled in Phrygia by the Emperor Theodosius (379-395 A.D.) soon thereafter revolted, paring and pillaging throughout Asia Minor. In 399 A.D. Selge, too, was attacked by Goths under the leadership of Tribigild, but beat the enemy back. This show of force is proof that Selge had lost none of its former strength.

Selge lay on three hills surrounded by a for-

A Roman bridge over Köprüçay river

tification wall. This wall, of which a portion survives today, had seven main entrances and high towers spaced at intervals averaging 100 metres. The first ruin visible today is the Greco-Roman type theatre, which forms part of the modern day village of Zerk. The theatre's lower portion rests on a rocky slope. The horseshoeshaped cavea is cut by a diazoma dividing the theatre into 30 tiers of seats below and fifteen above. The first row immediately below the diazoma has kept its stone seats intact. This theatre had a seating capacity of about 9,000. Four separate entrances give onto the diazoma. In addition, vaulted paradoses running between the cavea and the stage also provide access to the theatre. The Roman period stage building survives today only as a heap of rubble. Its general outlines, however, can be made out; it had five doors and a collonnaded facade. It can be dated to the second century A.D.

Immediately to one side of the theatre one can trace the outlines of the opposing rows of seats belonging to the stadium, even though it is, on the whole, in a very ruinous state. It appears from the surviving portions that the stadium was in all likelihood a little smaller than average. There are also several surviving inscriptions recording victories in the stadium at Selge. Most of these competitions were local, but every four years a larger regional festival and competitions took place.

The remains of two temples can be found atop the highest hill to the west. It is more than likely that this is the Kesbedion mentioned by Polybios. In that case, the large 17x34 metre peripteral temple must have been that of the city's chief god, Zeus. As for the small temple with the templum in antis plan, this can be tentatively assigned to Artemis on the basis of an inscription found nearby.

Behind this hill is a giant round cistern, built not only for rainwater, but also to hold water brought by a channel coming from the northwest.

Between this hill and the other hills to the south-east, lie the other principal municipal buildings. Here on an incline lie the extremely fragmentary remains of a very long porticoed street, a nymphaeum, and a bath.

On top of the hill to the south-east lie the remains of a large square plan agora enclosed on three sides. Attached to it is an apsidal basilica belonging to a later period.

The ruins of Selge which mostly date from the Roman period show that, especially in the 2nd century A.D. Selge was a wealthy and influential city.

Selge remains unexcavated.

Rafting on Köprüçay River

Another bridge over Köprüçay river